D1506041

# WORLD OF COLORS

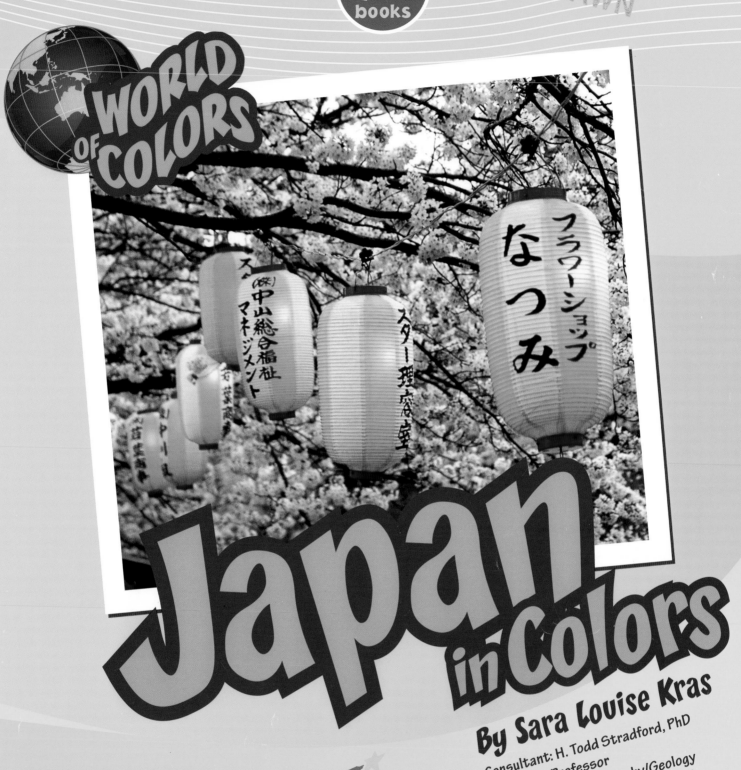

フラワーショップ
なつみ

# Japan in Colors

By Sara Louise Kras

Consultant: H. Todd Stradford, PhD
Associate Professor
Department of Geography/Geology
University of Wisconsin, Platteville

Capstone press®
Mankato, Minnesota

**Golden** fur frames the bright **red** faces of these Japanese macaques. Japanese macaques are also called snow monkeys. They live in the mountains and forests of Japan. In the winter, they squeeze together to keep warm.

**White** snow blankets the top of Mount Fuji. Mount Fuji is the tallest mountain in Japan. Thousands of people climb to the top each year.

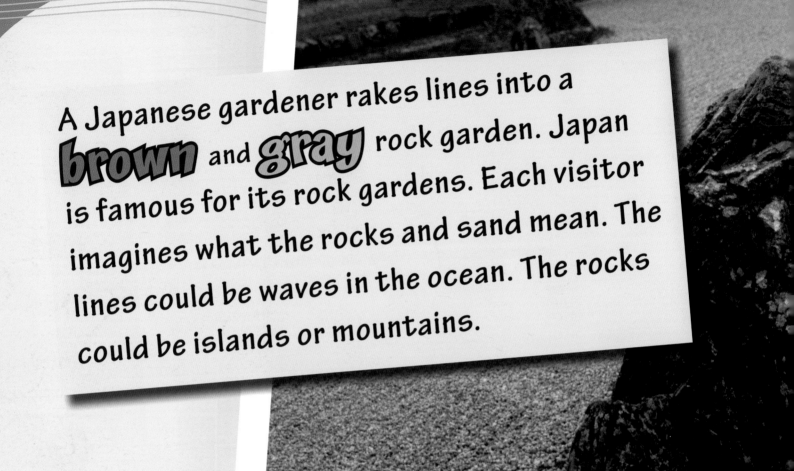

A Japanese gardener rakes lines into a **brown** and **gray** rock garden. Japan is famous for its rock gardens. Each visitor imagines what the rocks and sand mean. The lines could be waves in the ocean. The rocks could be islands or mountains.

**White**, **green**, and **orange** pieces of sushi sit on a bamboo tray. Sushi is a popular food in Japan. It's filled with rice, vegetables, and raw fish. The Japanese eat sushi with chopsticks. They dip the pieces in soy sauce and a mustard called wasabi.

Rows of tea plants paint the land green. Workers pick the leaves and take them to a factory. The leaves are then steamed, rolled, and dried. Green tea is a popular drink in Japan.

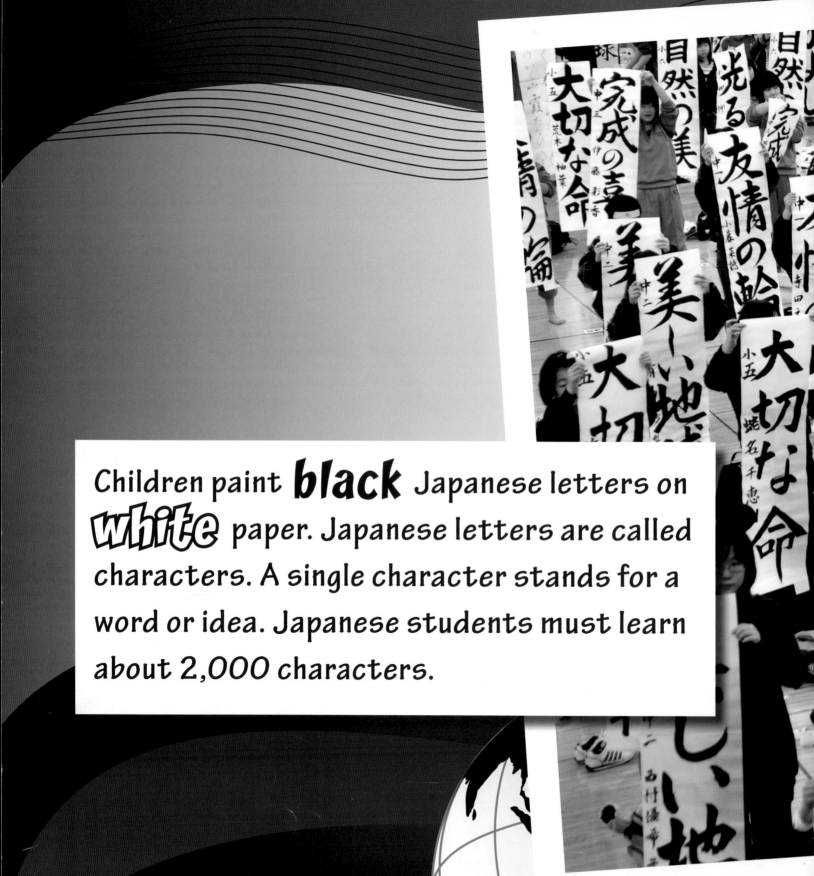

Children paint **black** Japanese letters on **white** paper. Japanese letters are called characters. A single character stands for a word or idea. Japanese students must learn about 2,000 characters.

Geisha dancers perform in **yellow**, **red**, and **blue** kimonos. A kimono is a robe made from silk. It is tied around the waist with a sash called an obi. Japanese women wear kimonos on holidays and at weddings. Some wear them for everyday dress.

**Purple** origami animals show the Japanese art of paper folding. Origami artists begin with a square piece of colored paper. Then they fold the paper into an animal, flower, or other fun shape.

A **white** Japanese robot plays a **brown** violin. Japan is a world leader in building robots. Thousands of robots work in Japan. Many of them work in factories. Robots build cars, plant rice, and serve sushi. They even build other robots!

Cherry trees burst with **pink** blossoms in spring. The Japanese look forward to spring after a cold, snowy winter. They have picnics and rest below the beautiful trees. The Japanese make the most of spring weather before the hot, humid summer.

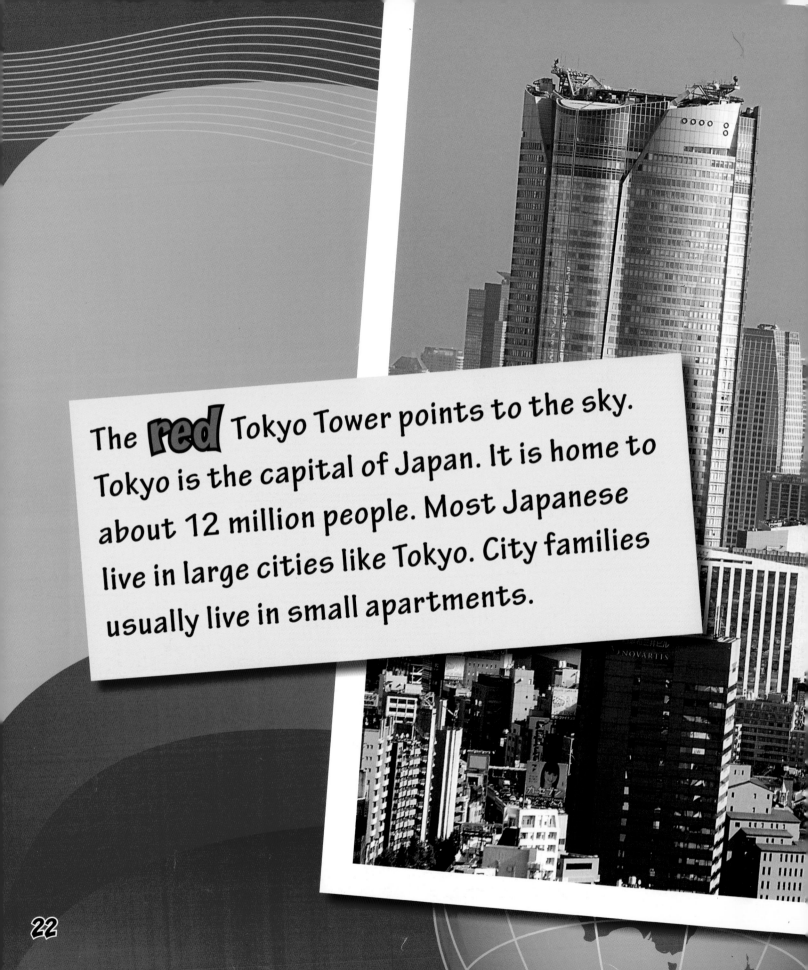

The **red** Tokyo Tower points to the sky. Tokyo is the capital of Japan. It is home to about 12 million people. Most Japanese live in large cities like Tokyo. City families usually live in small apartments.

Buddhist priests ring a **gray** bell to celebrate the Japanese New Year. Priests hit the bell to wash away the past and start the year fresh. The New Year is the largest celebration in Japan.

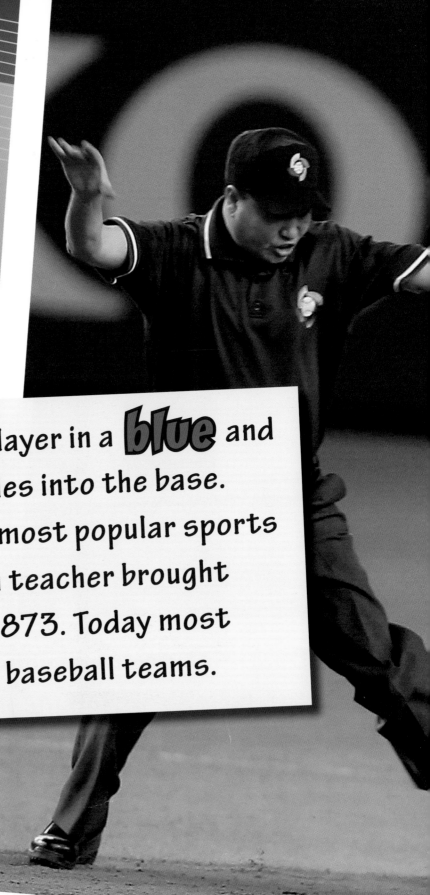

A Japanese baseball player in a **blue** and **white** uniform slides into the base. Baseball is one of the most popular sports in Japan. An American teacher brought baseball to Japan in 1873. Today most schools in Japan have baseball teams.

# FACTS about Japan

**Capital City:** Tokyo

**Population:** 127,288,416

**Official Language:** Japanese

## Common Phrases

| English | Japanese | Pronunciation |
|---------|----------|---------------|
| hello | kon ni chi wa | (koh-NEE-chee-wah) |
| good-bye | sayonara | (sah-yo-NAH-rah) |
| yes | ha i | (HYE) |
| no | i i e | (EE-ay) |

## Map

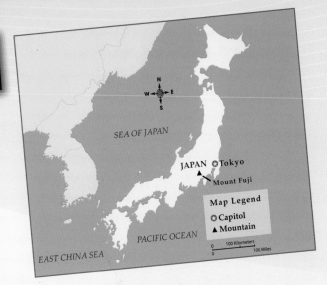

## Flag

## Money

Japanese money is called the yen.

# Glossary

**Buddhist** (BOO-dist) — a person who follows the religion of Buddhism; Buddhism is based on the teachings of Buddha; Buddhists believe that people may live many lives in different bodies.

**geisha** (GEI-shaw) — a Japanese girl or woman who is trained to provide entertainment and company

**kimono** (kee-MOH-noh) — a long, loose robe with wide sleeves and a sash

**macaque** (muh-KAK) — an Asian monkey; the Japanese macaque is the only kind of primate that can live in very cold regions.

**obi** (OH-bee) — a Japanese sash worn with a kimono

**origami** (or-uh-GAH-mee) — the Japanese art of paper folding

**soy** (SOI) — a dark liquid that is made from soybeans; soy is used as a sauce to flavor food.

**sushi** (SOO-shee) — a meal made of vegetables, raw fish, and cold, cooked rice

**wasabi** (wah-SAH-bee) — a pastelike substance made from the root of an Asian mustard plant; wasabi tastes similar to horseradish.

# Read More

Burgan, Michael. *Japan*. Questions and Answers. Countries. Mankato, Minn.: Capstone Press, 2005.

Kalman, Bobbie. *Japan the People*. The Lands, Peoples, and Cultures Series. New York: Crabtree, 2008.

Streissguth, Tom. *Japan*. Country Explorers. Minneapolis: Lerner, 2008.

# Internet Sites

FactHound offers a safe, fun way to find educator-approved Internet sites related to this book.

Here's what you do:

1. Visit *www.facthound.com*

2. Choose your grade level.

3. Begin your search.

This book's ID number is 9781429622240.

FactHound will fetch the best sites for you!

# Index

A+ Books are published by Capstone Press,
151 Good Counsel Drive, P.O. Box 669, Mankato, Minnesota 56002.
www.capstonepress.com

1 2 3 4 5 6 14 13 12 11 10 09

*Library of Congress Cataloging-in-Publication Data*
Kras, Sara Louise.
    Japan in colors / by Sara Louise Kras.
    p. cm. — (A+ books. World of colors)
Includes bibliographical references and index.
    Summary: "Simple text and striking photographs present Japan, its culture, and its
geography" — Provided by publisher.
    ISBN-13: 978-1-4296-2224-0 (hardcover)
    ISBN-10: 1-4296-2224-5 (hardcover)
    1. Japan — Juvenile literature. 2. Japan — Pictorial works — Juvenile literature. I. Title.
II. Series.
DS806.K78 2009                                           2008034125
952 — dc22

**Credits**
Megan Peterson, editor; Veronica Bianchini, set designer; Kyle Grenz, book designer;
    Wanda Winch, photo researcher

**Photo Credits**
Alamy/Chad Ehlers, 10–11; AP Images/Katsumi Kasahara, 13; Art Life Images/
age fotostock/Frank Carter, 14–15; Art Life Images/age fotostock/Japack, 4–5; Art
Life Images/age fotostock/Jose Fuste Raga, 22–23; Capstone Press, 29 (banknote);
Capstone Press/Karon Dubke, 8–9, 16–17; Getty Images Inc./Koichi Kamoshida,
26–27; Getty Images Inc./Reportage/Eightfish, 6–7; Landov LLC/Bloomberg News/
Kimimasa Mayama, 18–19; Landov LLC/Kyodo, 24–25; Shutterstock, 20–21;
Shutterstock/Arteki, 29 (flag); Shutterstock/Laitr Keiows, 29 (coins); Shutterstock/
Michael Nguyen, cover; Shutterstock/mypokcik, 1; Shutterstock/WizData, Inc., 2–3

**Note to Parents, Teachers, and Librarians**
This World of Colors book uses full-color photographs and a nonfiction format to introduce children
to basic topics in the study of countries. *Japan in Colors* is designed to be read aloud to a
pre-reader or to be read independently by an early reader. Photographs help listeners and early
readers understand the text and concepts discussed. The book encourages further learning by
including the following sections: Facts about Japan, Glossary, Read More, Internet Sites, and Index.
Early readers may need assistance using these features.